Peterborough
in old picture postcards

by Allan Bunch

European Library   ZALTBOMMEL/THE NETHERLANDS

GB ISBN 90 288 6358 3

© 1996 European Library – Zaltbommel/The Netherlands

Introduction

Early communities have existed in the Peterborough area since 4000 B.C. and the evidence can be seen at the Flag Fen museum in Fengate. The Romans also built a major pottery and town at nearby Castor (Durobrivae). A monastic foundation was established in the 7th century during the Saxon period and it was usual for a market and dwellings to develop outside the monastery walls. However, the earliest record of a city exisiting separately from the monastery was in 1070 when Hereward and the Danes set fire to it and the monastery in a successful attempt to stop the abbey's treasures falling into the hands of the Normans. The town at this time was on the east side of the monastery in the area of Boongate.

With the building of a new Abbey church from 1118, the centre of Burgh (as it was then called) was moved to the west side of the church. A new Marketstede was laid out and roads grew around it, forming the basis of the present town centre. Communications with the outside world were helped immensely by the building of a wooden bridge across the River Nene in 1308. During this period Burgh became Burgh St. Peter and later Peterborough, taking its name from the dedication of the Abbey church to St. Peter. With the dissolution of the Abbey by Henry VIII in 1539 and the creation of a bishopric, Peterborough became a city. The administration of the city was shared between the Dean and Chapter of the Cathedral as Lords of the Manor; the magistrates, who were appointed by the Lord Paramount of Peterborough (Lord Burghley) and responsible for law and order; and the Churchwardens (later the Feoffees) who maintained the upkeep of public buildings, highways and bridges. It was during this period also that the celebrated gravedigger Robert Scarlett buried two Queens in the Cathedral – Henry's wife Katherine of Aragon and Mary, Queen of Scots.

The city developed little over the next two centuries, its extent being from the river to City Road – Midgate – Westgate in one direction and from Boongate to the line of the present railway in the other. During the Civil War Colonel Richard Cromwell's soldiers knocked the Cathedral about a bit, smashed the stained glass and destroyed precious charters and other records. The Restoration of Charles II was marked with the building of the Guildhall in the Market Place as a venue for meetings of the Feoffees and other public events. The establishment of Improvement Commissioners in the 1790s, with powers to raise taxes, led to a vast improvement to the city's streets and encouraged the flow of wheeled traffic. Peterborough at this time still remained predominantly a market town with industry very much agriculture based.

As one Victorian travel writer put it, an 'accident of situation' in the mid-19th century led to Peterborough becoming a major rail centre at the crossing point of lines from the Midlands to East Anglia and London to the north. This sparked off the first major development and growth of the city. New estates were built to house the railway workers, engineering industries developed, and the embryo brickmaking industry, located on the Oxford Clay beds south of the city, expanded to cope with a nationwide boom in building. Commence and trade flourished as improved public transport – trains, carriers' carts, horse buses, and trams – attracted people from surrounding villages to the city. Even river traffic, that might have been expected to decline, increased for a time as goods were transferred from rail to barge for onward transmission to the coast. In just twenty years, from 1841 to 1861, the city's population increased from 7,125 to 11,732.

In 1874 the city was incorporated as a municipal borough and the foundations of modern local government were set. Police and fire services were developed, electricity, piped water and sewerage systems were provided, schools and libraries built. As Peterborough continued to grow throughout the 20th century, emphasis changed from agriculture to engineering. The railway companies, Baker Perkins, Peter Brotherhoods, London Brick and Perkins Engines being some of the major employers.

This book of photographs captures the city during the period of its first expansion, from the 1850s to 1930. The second major expansion in the 1970s and 80s, when Peterborough was developed as a New Town and effectively doubled in size, has swept away many of the old buildings and some of the ancient streets. Some buildings have been sensitively preserved but much of value has been lost. In these photographs you will see a reminder of what has gone and, perhaps, identify what remains, though often hidden behind a modern facade. You will also find here details of some of the people who helped to shape the city.

I am greatly indebted to the knowledge and help of Richard Hillier, Local History Librarian at Peterborough Central Library and to Cambridgeshire Libraries for permission to use the photographs from their collection. Many thanks also to H.J.K. Jenkins for information on Fenland lighters. I have also found the following works extremely useful: H.F. Tebbs, Peterborough: a history, 1979; H.F. Tebbs, How the city has changed, 1975; Donald Mackreth, Peterborough: history and guide, 1994; Leslie Webb, Some Peterborough buildings, 1986; and Mary Liquorice, ed., Posh folk, 1991.

1   We begin our pictorial journey through old Peterborough with the magnificent Cathedral at the heart of the city. There has been a place of worship on this site since Peada, King of Mercia, is credited with founding the first abbey in 655. This was sacked by the Danes in 870 and refounded as a Benedictine Abbey by Aethelwold, Bishop of Winchester, in 960. Two years after the accidental destruction of the second Abbey by fire in 1116, Abbot John de Sais began the work on the present building. With various additions, this was finally completed in 1508. Here we see the soaring west front, said to be unique in Christendom for marrying the Classical idea of a portico with Gothic style. The Perpendicular porch was added in 1380 to stop the forward lean of the central arch.

49 West Front, Peterborough Cathedral

2   Entering the Cathedral by the west door, you are met by this splendid view of the great Norman nave built between 1160 and 1185, largely at the instigation of Abbot Benedict, who came to Peterborough from Canterbury. The painted wooden ceiling is one of the special features of this Cathedral and there is no comparable example in England. It is made up of diamond shaped lozenges containing medieval symbolic images and decoration reminiscent of illuminated manuscripts of the period.

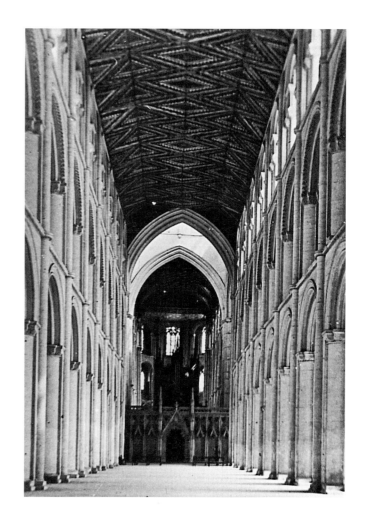

3 Past the nave, the choir stalls and the transepts lies the most complete Norman apse surviving in England, built between 1118 and 1140. The ornate ceiling was designed about 1860 by Sir George Gilbert Scott (1811-1878), the leading architect of the mid-19th century Gothic revival. It is based on a description of the original medieval ceiling destroyed by Cromwell's soldiers in 1643. Sir George Gilbert Scott was responsible for the design of the Albert Memorial, the Foreign Office, and St. Pancras Station in London, and of Peterscourt in Peterborough (see illustration 37).

4   Beyond the apse is what is referred to, relatively, as the New Building, being the last major construction work on the Cathedral. It was commissioned by Abbot Robert Kirkton and built between 1496 and 1508. The architect was almost certainly John Wastell, who also built the central tower of Canterbury Cathedral and King's College Chapel, Cambridge. Here we catch a glimpse of his delicate stonework of the fan vaulting.

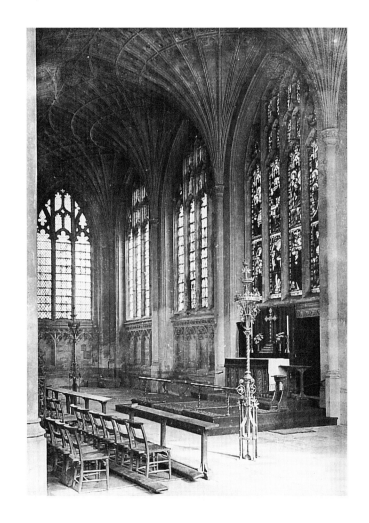

5   This very early photograph of the east end of the Cathedral is believed to be taken from Fengate Lane (approximately where Bishop Creighton School is now) sometime in 1850s. It captures a moment of stillness as a carrier takes a respite from his labours. It also demonstrates the rural nature of Peterborough in those days, a time that was soon to change with the recently arrived railways. However, even today, a feeling of that stillness can still be found by leaving the busy city centre behind and entering the Cathedral precincts.

6   North of the west front in the monastic building was the Prior's Lodging. Little remains of the original building except for the hall which still exists, though heavily restored, as the Chapter House. However, this splendid Tudor gateway is still there to be admired. In this postcard it is described as Kirkton's Gate, after the abbot who had it build about 1500, though it is now usually referred to as Prior's Gate. The gateway is decorated with many flattering Tudor symbols and you will also find the abbot's distinctive rebus (a visual pun on his name) of a church (kirk) and a barrel (tun).

Peterborough Cathedral, Kirkton's Gate.

7   We leave the Cathedral by its great Norman gateway seen here in around 1900. It was built by Abbot Benedict circa 1180. Above the gate is the Norman Chapel of St. Nicholas and to the right is the printing office formerly of Joseph S. Clarke, who founded the *Peterborough Advertiser* in 1854. The building housing the printing office was demolished when Narrow Street was widened in the 1920's.

8   Emerging from the Cathedral immediately in front of you is the wide open space of the Market Place (now Cathedral Square) seen here about 1894. In the centre on the opposite side of the Square is the Guildhall, also referred to in the past as the Market Cross or Butter Cross. It has changed little over the years, though the buildings to the right of it have disappeared to be replaced by underground public toilets. At this time they housed William Bell, an itinerant tea dealer, Robert Back, a watchmaker, and various city officers, such as the Borough Surveyor, Waterworks Engineer, and Borough Overseer and Collector. Behind these buildings can be seen the tower of St. John's parish church.

9   The Guildhall was built in 1671 by public subscription to commemorate the restoration of King Charles II, probably over the site of an early village cross and later a single-storey, arcaded building. It was erected to provide shelter for the market people and the rooms above have been used for a variety of functions over the years, including a school, public lectures, auctions, public balls, dancing classes, a court room, and for occasional meetings of the Feoffees (an early form of city council). The Royal Arms under the clock were placed there in fulfilment of a condition attached to a gift of £20 made by Lord Fitzwilliam to the building fund.

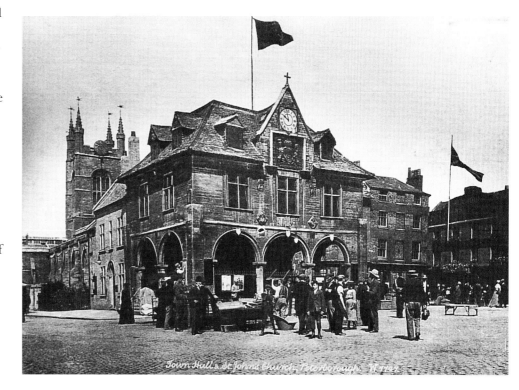

10 From this angle it can be seen that there was originally a building abutting the Guildhall at the rear and facing onto Church Street. This was the Town Clerk's office and also the access point to the upper floors of the Guildhall. Hereby hangs a mystery. This building is of later construction than the Guildhall and, when demolished in the 1950s, there was an expectation of finding evidence of how people accessed the upper floors of the Guildhall before the extension was built. However, none came to light and the present metal spiral staircases were added.

11   A very different picture of the Market Place from that in illustration 8, taken about the same time. Now it contains all the activity of the Saturday market, whose long history stretches back over 1000 years. In 972 A.D. King Edgar granted rights to the Abbot of Peterborough for a market and a mint. For almost 200 years the market was sited in Boongate but, following a westward expansion of the town, it was moved opposite the great gate of the Cathedral. The market was originally only held on Saturdays but, as the city expanded, a Wednesday market developed from 1838.

12   Crockery and iron-mongery stall, about 1890. With the expansion of the city, the Market Place became inadequate to contain all the activity and it spilled over into the surrounding streets. Certain streets came to be associated with particular produce or business e.g. Cumbergate for pigs and hides and Church Street for fish and poultry. Butter was sold under the Guildhall (usually referred to as the Butter Cross until the 1920s), loose cattle and penned sheep in Long Causeway and meat, west of St. John's Church. In 1863, the cattle market was moved to a new site east of Broadway now partly occupied by *The Academy* and Tesco's supermarket. The general market remained in the Market Place until the early 1960s when it moved to its present site on the closure of the cattle market.

At the same time Market Place was renamed Cathedral Square.

13   Fish market, outside the Town Clerk's Office in Church Street circa 1900. Its proximity to St. John's Church brought complaints from those attending Sunday services that they could still smell Saturday's fish. In the background is the Butter Market taking place under the Guildhall (Butter Cross), where women sold butter, eggs and poultry. Two or three times a year, the Butter Cross gates were locked and all the butter weighed. Any that was underweight was taken away and believed to have been given to the poor. When the Guildhall was renovated in 1927 and the gates taken away, the last of the 'butter-women', a Mrs. Bellairs, was found a stall on the general market.

14   Another view of Cathedral Square in the early 1900s, this time looking east from the Guildhall towards the Cathedral gate. In the centre of the picture is the Gates Memorial erected in 1897 in memory of the city's first Mayor, Henry Pearson Gates who died in 1893. It also had its uses, being equipped with four taps and granite basins. When the Market Place was renamed Cathedral Square in the early 1960s, the memorial was moved to Bishop's Road Gardens, minus plinth, taps and basins.

15   St. John's Church, seen here from the Cowgate/Cross Street junction, is the parish church of Peterborough. It replaced an earlier 13th century church located in the Boongate area east of the Cathedral. As the town developed westward, the church was eventually relocated in the early 15th century to its present site, outstaring the Cathedral across the Market Place. The reason for the church standing in a hollow is said to be because the area had formerly been used by butchers to slaughter animals, and the ground had become contaminated with blood. This had to be dug out before the church could be built on pure ground. Also in this picture, on the extreme left is the Corn Exchange and next to it an ale-house and offices of the Newark brewers Warwick and Richardson.

16 The tower of St. John's originally had a spire, but this was removed in the late 1820s as it had become unsafe. In 1976 the church clock face was removed, putting an end to the old Peterborough saying: 'When the church clock and the Abbey clock strike both together, There will soon be a death or a change in the weather.' I suppose nowadays that's what one might call a fairly sure bet! A carillon was added in 1857 and can still be heard several times a day playing such songs as *The Bluebells of Scotland*. On the right of the photograph is the town pump which remained there long after the city had piped water supply, being particularly useful to the market traders.

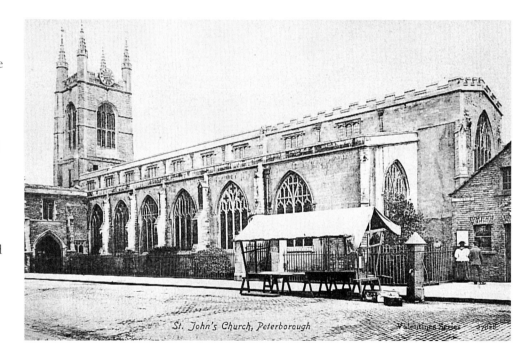

St. John's Church, Peterborough

Valentines Series

17   Turning left out of the Cathedral gateway brings you into Bridge Street which was originally in two parts. The stretch down to present-day Woolworth's and the Bourges Boulevard crossing was known as Narrow Street (or Narrow Bridge Street) and the section down to the river and Town Bridge was Broad Bridge Street, so named because it was effectively twice the width of Narrow Street, which even at its widest point was only twenty feet from kerb to kerb. Here we see it around the turn of the century in a delightful drawing made by Kate Colman, the daughter of Samuel Colman, co-owner of Cadge and Colman's flour mill on the south bank of the river.

18　A photographic view this time of the entrance to Narrow Street from the Market Place between 1898 and 1901. Central to the picture is the inappropriately named building 'The Louvre'. It belonged to Jenner Jermyn & Co., Ltd., drapers, milliners, dressmakers, carpet factors and sewing machine agents. The building is being demolished to make way for the London, City and Midland Bank which is still on the site but now known more succinctly as the Midland Bank. Perhaps Jermyn's would have had more success by building a glass pyramid in the middle of Market Place? On the left, at the entrance to Narrow Street, is J.H. Pearson's chemist shop, also home to A.E. Quarterman, artificial teeth maker, and next to it the Universal Tea Company. It is not known whether the tea pickers' baskets hanging on the outside of the building were for display or sale.

19   Another view of the west side of Narrow Street at the turn of the century. The large clock projecting from Paviour's jewelry shop may be familiar. It is of a type known as a 'skeleton clock', that is the mechanism is some distance away from the clock face, the fingers being operated by a series of rods and linkages. In 1929, around the time Narrow Street was widened to bring it into line with Broad Bridge Street, the clock was moved to the old Carnegie Central Library in Broadway (now Rinaldo's night club). The clock became one of the few working examples of its type on a public building. Its active service days ceased in 1990 when the library moved to its new premises on the opposite corner of Fitzwilliam Street and Broadway. The mechanism was removed to the City Museum for preservation but the clock face remains, powered now by an electric motor.

20   This photograph of the well-known Peterborough establishment of Pentney, Printers and Stationers can be accurately dated to 1898 from the billboards announcing the imminent demise of the great British prime minister William Ewart Gladstone. The Pentney firm began as a sideline of the Reverend W. Pentney, who set up as a bookseller in cottages in front of his chapel. Later, he purchased John Harley's printing establishment situated in the attics of the Guildhall. The whole business moved to Narrow Street in 1860. His son, William Henry Pentney joined the business, eventually rising to become manager. The premises remained in Narrow Street until it was widened, whence it removed to 9 Church Street, continuing there until the 1950s.

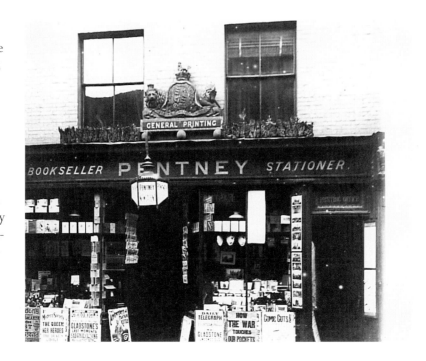

21　The Cross Keys Inn stood on the east side of Narrow Street on the site now occupied by the Town Hall. It was regarded as the oldest licensed premises in Peterborough and was demolished on the widening of Narrow Street in the 1920s.

22 In 1492 Abbot William de Ramsey let to Richard Wyvill one hostelry with the sign of the Angel next to the corner of Priestgate. And there the Angel Hotel remained for over five hundred years when it was demolished to make way for W.H. Smiths. In the 18th century it became the sporting centre of the city. Entries for the Peterborough Horse Races had to be recorded at the *Angel* and cockfighting continued there for several years after the sport had been banned. In the 19th century it became the centre for local Tory politics and, at election time, was a target for blazing tar-barrels and, on one occasion, a blazing cab (see illustration 103).

23   Moving into Broad Bridge Street now, this busy scene looking towards Narrow Street emphasises the difference in width between the two, an effect that is possibly the result of the course of an ancient stream flowing from Swans Pool into the Nene (see also illustration 31). Leading to the right in front of the *Golden Lion* is Bishop's Road, now part of the busy inner-city ring road. The *Golden Lion* dates from the late 18th century. It later became Murkett's Garage before being demolished in the 1920s. The Salvation Army used to hold services at this spot every Saturday night, summer and winter.

24 Another view of Nar-
ror Street from Broad
Bridge Street towards the
end of the 19th century. Immediately on the left is the
Wagon and Horses inn (where
Woolworth's now stands).
The huge padlock you can
see further along was the
shop sign of ironmongers
Plumpton and Petts.

25   Taking a short detour down Bishop's Road, soon brings us to Bishop's Gardens. The attractive, half-timbered building, originally called St. Oswald's Close (now St. Peter's House), was the home of Florence Saunders. She was the youngest daughter of Augustus Page Saunders (Dean of Peterborough from 1853-1878) and was one of the first ladies to take a professional interest in nursing. After training at the Evelina Hospital in London, she returned to Peterborough and devoted herself to the nursing of working class invalids in their own homes. In 1884 she founded the Peterborough District Nursing Association and her own home became its headquarters. After her death in 1904, the Association was renamed The Florence Saunders Nursing Association. The building remained a nurses' home until 1974 when the accommodation became unsuitable by modern standards and was closed. It is now used as offices.

Peterborough   Bishop's Gardens

The Wrench Series No. 3998

26   Returning to Broad Bridge Street, this is the view looking towards the river with *The Boat Inn* and *The Rose and Crown Inn* on the left. Bridge Street before the bridge was built had original been called Hythegate, because it led to the hythe or wharf. When the first bridge was erected in 1308, its name changed to High-gate and later Bridge Street.

27 Continuing south, we shortly reach the River Nene and the Town Bridge. The first bridge to cross the Nene was built by the Abbot of Peterborough in 1308 to replace the existing ford. It was a timber bridge on stone piers that lasted, with various rebuildings and repairs, until 1872 when it was replaced by an iron structure. Until modern times the upkeep of the bridge depended largely on charity, with responsibility frequently disputed.

28   The iron Town Bridge, which replaced the ancient wooden structure in 1872, was paid for by public subscription. It lasted until 1934 when the present concrete bridge was built, effectively doubling the width of the road and extending as a viaduct over the railway line. The crowds seen here on the new bridge are either testing its strength or, more likely, watching a rowing race taking place on the river.

29   Situated on the north bank of the river beside the Town Bridge is the so-called Customs House, though there is little evidence that it was used as such. The present building dates from the early 18th century but there has probably been a building on this site since the middle ages. In the late 19th century it was used as a coal wharf but is now more appropriately the headquarters of Peterborough Sea Scouts.

30   This view of the Nene looking downstream from the Town Bridge shows what the river looked like before being put in a straight-jacket of embanking. Whilst certainly reducing the incidence of flooding, it nevertheless destroyed much of the river's picturesqueness.

RIVER NENE FROM BRIDGE, PETERBOROUGH.

31 Tracing our steps back to Market Square and continuing northwards past the Cathedral brings us to Long Causeway, its name is a reference to the fact that a stream once ran down the middle of it. This may account for the street being wider than usual, since tracks developed on both sides of the stream. Eventually the stream was diverted or filled in leaving a double width road. J.W. Bodger, who took this photograph, was a prominent figure in Peterborough for many decades. We shall meet him again in illustration 52.

LONG CAUSEWAY, PETERBOROUGH.

J. W. Bodger, Peterborough and Hunstanton.

32   This view of the northern end of Long Causeway was taken before 1904. You can see that the continuation north (now Broadway) was partially blocked by buildings. The narrower road to the left led to the Cattle Market. Broadway itself originally ended round about Fitzwilliam Street. It was then widened and aligned with Long Causeway in 1904-05.

LONG CAUSEWAY.   PETERBOROUGH.

33   The building partially blocking the end of Long Causeway had originally been a 17th century house and, over the years, a vicarage and a solicitor's office. At the time of this photograph it is in the hands of a photographer with a strong desire to ensure that we get the message 'They've all got sticky backs'! 'Sticky Backs' were the forerunner of Polyfotos – a series of snaps taken in rapid succession with, presumably, having adhesive backs to facilitate their being mounted in albums or on calling cards. The corny sign above the door would, no doubt, be deemed politically incorrect these days.

34   Looking back along Long Causeway from its junction with Midgate and Westgate, we see on opposite corners of the road, stores belonging to Thomas Lawrence Barrett. He was one of the most important figures in the city's commercial life. Twice mayor of the city and a J.P., he began as an apprentice draper at the age of 14 and ended up as owner of stores employing one hundred people. The Midgate corner drapery store opened in 1884. It was a four-storey building, the upper floors containing bedrooms and a dormitory where he and his staff lived in. Barrett was one of the first business owners in Peterborough to install electric lighting. He also bought one of the first gramophones to be seen in the city, and proudly showed it off in the hall of the shop by playing music to his customers. Later Barrett opened another store on the opposite corner selling furniture, carpets and grocery. The stores closed in 1965, the Midgate one standing empty for eight years before being demolished to make way for Midgate House, a modern block of shops and offices. The Westgate corner building is still standing.

LONG CAUSEWAY, PETERBOROUGH

35 Turning right at the end of Long Causeway brings us into Midgate. This was originally called Howegate, a reference to the 'howe' or mound known as Tout Hill, on which stood a castle built by Abbot Thurold to defend the Cathedral against further raids by Hereward the Wake. This view is of the north side of Midgate in the 1890s showing from the left of the photograph: Edmund Gill's china warehouse; Stephen Stanley the butcher; the *Wheatsheaf* pub; Herbert Kemp, watchmaker; Watson's 'Boot Market'; and the Swan Inn sign just visible beyond. Note the two examples of dogcarts, a popular form of personal transport in the 19th and early 20th century.

36   The Swan Inn, Midgate, a paricularly fine example of 17th century architecture, seen here prior to re-fronting in 1897. *The Swan* is said to have been one of the starting points for the Peterborough Dilligence coach which left at five in the morning for Holborn in London. A later landlord of *The Swan*, William Bailey, ran a fleet of horse-drawn omnibuses that served all the local villages. Unfortunately Abbot Thurold's castle was no longer around to protect *The Swan* from the much later deprevations of another Hereward, the Hereward Centre, and was demolished in the 1960s.

37   Further down, Midgate gives way to City Road and immediately on the right hand side lies this fine building designed by the famous architect of the Gothic Revival, Sir George Gilbert Scott. Known today as Peterscourt, it was originally built in 1859 by the Diocese of Peterborough as St. Peter's Teacher Training College for men. It continued as such until 1914 when it closed for the duration of the First World War, opening again in 1921 as a women's teacher training college. When the Guildhall in London was severely damaged in the blitz of 1940, the doorway was rescued and fixed in Peterscourt. After the Second World War it continued for a time in its original role but later was converted to offices and used by Perkins Engines and Peterborough Development Corporation amongst others.

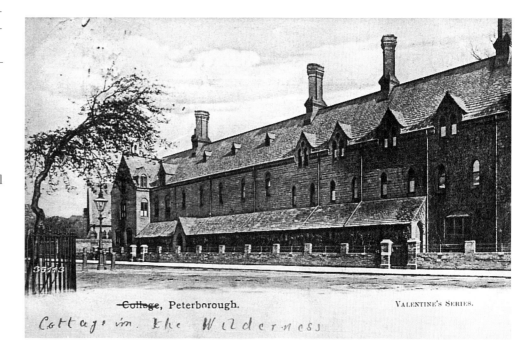

College, Peterborough.

VALENTINE'S SERIES.

Cottage in the Wilderness

38 Retracing our steps back to the junction with Long Causeway we turn north into Broadway, seen here post-1913. On the left is the *Broadway Electric Theatre* (later the *Broadway Kinema*), and beyond the Central Library and *Theatre Royal*. On the right hand side is the *Hippodrome* and before it the Peterborough Pavilion Roller Skating Rink. The Rink was opened in 1909 but only lasted a few years. It closed in 1913-14 and the building converted to Brainsby's motor-repair garage. The site is now occupied by Tesco's supermarket.

BROADWAY, PETERBOROUGH.

39   One man, without his dog, shepherds a flock of sheep past the old Central Library in Broadway on their way to the market. The Central Library was built in 1905 largely at the expense of millionaire American philanthropist Andrew Carnegie, who came himself to open the building on 29th May, 1906. Prior to this, the library had occupied the Fitzwilliam Hall in Park Road (near the back of the former Shelton's Department Store). In 1990 the library moved to a large modern building on the opposite corner of Fitzwilliam Street. The old building was converted into a nightclub and café and in the evening, depending on your view, is either exotically or luridly outlined in neon.

40 Here we see Stanley Jast, the first librarian of Peterborough Public Libraries from 1892-1898, posing with his bicycle in front of a busy market scene in Long Causeway. He was of Polish origin, his father having found refuge in England after fighting unsuccessfully on the side of the Hungarian army against the Austrians. Jast's full name was Jastrzebski but colleagues persuaded him to shorten it to Jast in 1895, as the apparently unpronounceable combination of letters might hinder his career. It was probably a wise move as Jast went on to reach great heights in the library profession. On Jast's death in 1944, his obituary in the *Library Association Record* described him as '...the most original thinker, the most inventive worker, the best speaker and the dominant character in librarianship in his day'.

41 Turning left at the end of Long Causeway brings us into Westgate. The name is believed to be a corruption of Webstergate, the area settled by Brabant weavers in the reign of Richard II. It also conveniently leads in a westerly direction! The building on the right, past the shops, is the early 18th century Mansion House, home of Matthew Wyldbore, M.P. for Peterborough in 1768. He left money in his will for the bells of St. John's to be rung annually on 15th March to commemorate, so the story goes, an occasion when he was lost in a mist over Flag Fen and was guided safely home by the sound of St. John's Church bells. A custom that has been revived again recently. His house was finally demolished in 1925/26.

42   Just beyond the Mansion House on the same side is one of Peterborough's most well-known hostelries, the *Bull Hotel*, built in the late 18th century. The frontage has changed little, although in 1900 the roof was heightened and rebuilt. Over the years the hotel has expanded into neighbouring properties and its grounds now extend as far north as Fitzwilliam Street. Sandy's Bar, at the back of the *Bull*, was said to be a meeting place for many of Peterborough's most memorable characters. It was also the site for a time of the city pound were stray animals were kept. Perhaps there was a connection? The domed building beyond the *Bull* is Westgate House, at the time a Conservative club, but now part of the Co-operative department store. In the distance can be seen the distinctive twin spires of the Congregational Church, nicknamed 'Lound' and 'Vergette', after the two men who had them added.

43 Beyond the Bull Hotel, just before the junction with Park Road, stood for many years this early branch of the well-known chain store Boots the Chemist, seen here about 1900. A few years later they moved to new premises in the Market Place built in a mock Elizabethan style. This building replaced one that had been the private home of the splendidly named tailor Harry Chippendale Clarabut and also Dandy's wine and spirit shop. This building still attracts attention and is now occupied by the fast food outlet Burger King.

44　A view of Westgate around 1910, taken from the junction with Park Road. On the right at 35 Westgate are the premises of Dr. T.J. Walker, the first native of Peterborough to be granted the Freedom of the City, which he received on his 80th birthday in 1915. He was a much loved figure in the town not only as a doctor and surgeon at the Peterborough Infirmary, but also as a gifted amateur actor, photographer, archae-ologist and local historian. He wrote the definitive work on the prisoner-of-war camp at Norman Cross. He died a year later in 1916.

WESTGATE, PETERBOROUGH.

45　We now take a brief glimpse at Park Road, looking back towards Westgate, sometime after 1906. On the right is the new Baptist Church and Barrass Memorial Hall which replaced the Queen Street premises destroyed by fire in 1905 (see illustration 102). Thomas Barrass was the Baptists' first pastor who took office in 1853. When he retired in 1900 the church had increased from 5 to 500 members and had flourishing daughter churches in outlying districts. The Barrass Memorial Hall has since been demolished and replaced with a modern office block. The remainder of the west side of Park Road is now taken up with the Co-operative Society's Westgate House department store. Such was the paucity of traffic in those days, the boys appear to be enjoying a game of cricket in the road.

S 1160　　PARK ROAD & BAPTIST CHAPEL PETERBOROUGH.

46   This view of the south side of Westgate shows the shop of James Harrison Smith, one of Peterborough's 'characters'. He came to the city from Uppingham in 1890 and opened Smith's Umbrella Hospital at 50 Westgate. He also cashed in on the national craze for sending and collecting postcards. Smith specialised in local views which he sold from his shop. As business boomed he opened another shop at 12 Westgate in 1913, next to Boots the Chemist. He became affectionately known as 'Postcard' Smith, the name he adopted to distinguish himself from five other Smiths who lived in Westgate.

47   Proceeding further down Westgate brings you, on the north side, to the junction with what used to be called Boroughbury but is now the end of Lincoln Road. The name is said to derive from Burgh Buri, the open fields of the town and also applied to the area around the old manor. The building on the right of this picture is Boroughbury Malting, photographed before 1898. It is all that remained of Squires Brewery that existed on the site until 1837, when much of it was demolished to make way for North Street.

48 A few yards further on along Boroughbury, between Fitzwilliam Street and Manor House Street, stood this so-called 17th century manor house, viewed here from the rear. It is more likely to have been simply a tenant farmer's house than a true manor house and was demolished in 1920 when Dr. Bonner built the present 'Manor House'.

49   This large monastic barn was part of the manorial farm laid out by the Abbot of Peterborough in the 12th century. The farm occupied an area encompassing the present day Craig Street, Lincoln Road, Fitzwilliam Street and Manor House Street. The barn was built by Abbot Adam of Boothby about 1320 and was constructed entirely of oak with stone rubble walls. It stood on the northern bank of a stream that flowed from Westwood into the Nene just west of the Key Theatre, on the south side of present day Church Street. Miraculously it survived until 1892 when speculators bought the land and perpetrated one of the worst acts of vandalism in the city by demolishing it, starting with the stone walls and several years later the timber framework. The stone is said to have been used to face the nearby row of attractive, Scottish-looking and sounding, Rothesay Villas on Lincoln Road. The Elwes Hall was built on the site but that, in turn, has now been demolished.

50   Returning to the Market Place, we now explore the streets exiting from the south west corner. First, Church Street, which runs westward as far as Queen Street on the right and Cross Street on the left, whence it progresses as Cowgate. This busy scene looks back along Church Street towards the Market Place on market day. The building on the left is the Corn Exchange built in 1846 on the site of the old theatre. By the end of the century it was held to be the busiest in England, with room for over 1,000 people in its market room. Its activities were largely brought to an end by a firebomb in 1942. You can also see in the street further along a cabbies' shelter, very necessary during inclement weather.

PETERBOROUGH
CORN EXCHANGE & CHURCH ST.

51	Cowgate and Church Street around 1914. The *Bell and Crown* inn was originally the home of the first master of Deacon's School. The school itself had been sited in Cowgate, but by the time of this photograph had moved to Crown Street (later renamed Deacon's Street and now submerged under the Queensgate Centre. (See also illustration 121.) Further along, on the corner with Queen Street, can be seen the Corn Exchange and beyond, St. John's Church. This stretch was originally called Butchers Row, a reflection of its use on market days for the sale of meat.

52   A view looking towards the end of Cowgate pre-1911. On the left is the chemist shop of J.W. Bodger. John William Bodger (1856-1939) qualified as a pharmacist in 1874. He was one of the founder members of the Peterborough Natural History, Scientific and Archaeological Society in 1871 and two years later became its Honorary Secretary, a post he held for nearly 66 years. Until 1880, the Society had nowhere to house its collections and they were kept in boxes under Mr. Bodger's bed. On the right of the picture can be seen Armstrong's furnishings shop, still there in 1996, though the business is up for sale. Just beyond it is the old parish cemetery, purchased by the Churchwardens from the Feoffees in 1805. It is now covered by the Crescent Bridge roundabout.

53 Running parallel to Cowgate on the south side from Narrow Street to the railway (now Bourges Boulevard) is Priestgate, one of the oldest streets in Peterborough. It goes back at least to the 12th century when Abbot Martin of Bec moved the centre of the town from Boongate to west of the Abbey. The origins of the name are unclear but may refer to an ancient track taken by the monks to Holywell in Longthorpe. From the 17th century Priestgate gained a reputation for being the 'aristocratic' part of town. Nowadays, its name might more appropriately be changed to Solicitorgate. This view of Priestgate after 1905 is taken from the junction with Cross Street, looking west. On the left of the picture can just be seen the end of Trinity Congregational Church, built as an extension to an existing house in 1865. It is now a solicitor's office. In front of the church is an example of Peterborough's first electric arc street lighting.

54   This fine Georgian residence was built in 1816 for Manchester-born Thomas Alderson Cooke, known affectionately as 'Squire' Cooke. He died in 1854 and the house was purchased by the 5th Earl Fitzwilliam in 1856. He offered it for use as the Peterborough Infirmary and it continued as such until the purpose built Peterborough and District War Memorial Hospital, on the corner of Thorpe Road and Midland Road, was opened in 1928. The old building was 'presented to the citizens of Peterborough' by Sir Percy Malcolm Stewart (Chairman of the London Brick Company) in 1931, to be run by Peter- borough Archaeological Society as a museum. In the 1960s they handed over the running of the Museum and Art Gallery to the City Council.

55 Running from the north-west corner of the Market Place is a short narrow street bordering the north side of St. John's Church. In fact, until the 1890s it was known as St. John's Street but is now called Exchange Street and runs into the remnants of Queen Street. In this early view of Exchange Street looking east from Queens Street, the buildings on the right from St. John's Church are the sexton's house and next to it the premises of Harry Eggborough, fish curer. On the extreme right of the photograph is the rear corner of the Corn Exchange. The passage you can see between the Corn Exchange and the houses, was known as Five Post Alley. It ran into Church Street and, guess what, there were five posts at the other end! It is now the anonymous passage between the Norwich Union Building and St. John's Church.

56   The western end of Exchange Street runs into Queen Street which linked Westgate with Church Street. On the corner, facing the Corn Exhange was the Bedford Temperance Hotel, seen here between 1905 and 1910. Just beyond the hotel can be seen the Drill Hall, the venue for many large public functions in the city. Apart from the buildings on the immediate left of the photograph, the rest is now under Queensgate. The angled wall of the C & A store, flanking the entrance to Queensgate, reflects the line of Queens Street.

57   A right-angled street linked Exchange Street and Long Causeway. This was Cumbergate, the street of the woolcombers who settled there in the 13th century. They have long disappeared and so has the eastern end of Cumbergate, seen here at the junction with Long Causeway pre-1900. It was devoured by the Queensgate Shopping Centre but much of the southern end has been preserved, forming an attractive 'heritage' entrance to Queensgate. In spite of its short length, Cumbergate boasted entrances to seven pubs. On Saturday it was lined by carriers' carts, whose horses were stabled at the inns. This display of agricultural implements was probably part of St. Peter's Fair ('Cherry Fair') or the Peterborough Show.

58   Only two of the pubs in Cumbergate survived, the *White Horse Inn* (now Jaegers) and *The Still*, for many years run by the Crisp family as a wine and spirit shop with licensed premises to the rear. *The Still* was located at the point where Cumbergate took a ninety degree turn at the southern end of Westgate Arcade. From this photograph, taken during renovations in the 1920s, there is evidence that the building goes back beyond the 19th century. Although within the Queensgate development area, after much public outcry it was preserved and has recently reopened under new management.

59   In 1833 the city's first Post Office was housed in a small room in Priestgate. As postal work increased, it moved to larger premises in Long Causeway and, in 1874, to these splendid purpose built premises in Cumbergate. This picture was taken after the buildings were extended in 1904 to add a new sorting office. The Post Office remained there until the Queensgate development began, when it moved to its present nondescript premises in the Norwich Union building in Church Street.

Post Office, Peterborough.

60   The south east side of Cumbergate shortly after 1907 showing Miss Pears' Almshouses, built in 1903 at the bequest of Miss Frances Pears, the daughter of a Peterborough draper, who died in 1901. They replaced some existing almshouses built in 1835 by the Feoffees of Peterborough on a site once occupied by the city's Moothall and the old Bridewell or House of Correction. The almshouses consisted of a pair of two-storey cottages in yellow brick, set back and flanked by two protruding stone buildings, enclosing a garden. Apart from the northern stone building and the garden, the rest of the buildings remain, being used for commercial purposes, as a café and, until this year (1996), an Italian restaurant.

61 A view of the south west side of Cumbergate, opposite Miss Pear's Almshouses, in 1890. The building on the right, between the two carts, now adjoins Queensgate. It dates from the 17th century and is possibly the only timber-framed building remaining in the city centre. It was converted into a House of Maintenance or Parish Workhouse in 1722. Appropriately, the building now (in 1996) houses a ladies' hair and beauty salon!

62   Before the coming of the railways and for some time afterwards the river Nene was an important artery for the transport of goods to and from Peterborough. Agricultural products, especially corn and malt were sent down river for transporting by coaster to the other ports around the country. Coal, timber, groceries and bale goods were imported for the inland-country. This trade was effected mainly by barges, known as Fenland lighters which, typically, had a wooden, double-ended hull about 13 metres long by 3 metres wide with a flat bottom and could carry a cargo of around 20 tonnes. A useful feature of the Fenland lighter was its economy of operation, achieved by linking several vessels into 'gangs', as in this photograph taken in the early 1900s. This allowed the lighters to be managed by just two men, one on the boats steering and one handling the horse on the towpath. Note the long steering pole which made it possible to control the whole gang. The second lighter in the 'gang' has a chimney and this was probably a 'house' lighter which provided primitive kennel-like accommodation for overnight stays. This 'gang' probably belonged to the Freears of Stanground.

63   The coming of the railways, if not immediately, sounded the death knell for barge traffic. The first railway to reach Peterborough was the London and Birmingham Railway's Blisworth branch in 1845, linking Peterborough to Northampton via Wellingborough, Thrapston, Oundle, and Wansford. Originally a station was planned on the Fair Meadow but, through a deal with Eastern Counties Railway, who were planning to bring a line to the city from Ely, the ECR agreed to build a station on the south side of the river, east of the Town Bridge to accommodate both lines. Here we see a print of the East Station shortly after it was built in 1845, described by one writer as 'outside... like the relic of a Greek temple'. It fell a victim to Dr. Beeching's axe in 1966 and was demolished in 1972.

RAILWAY STATION, PETERBOROUGH.
Drawn & Engraved for the British Gazetteer

64   The Great Northern line from London to Peterborough was masterminded by Thomas Brassey, whose ancestors later came to live in the area at Apethorpe Hall. One of the biggest obstacles to the line was the boggy fenland of Whittlesea Mere. The solution was to sink rafts of wooden logs covered with peat along the path of the line. This was repeated over and over again until all the water was squeezed out and a firm foundation remained. The line then made a spectacular entry into Peterborough crossing the Nene and rival railways' lines on a bridge of sixteen graceful spans. It was the finest bridge that Peterborians had ever seen and prints, such as this one, were immediately struck and put on sale.

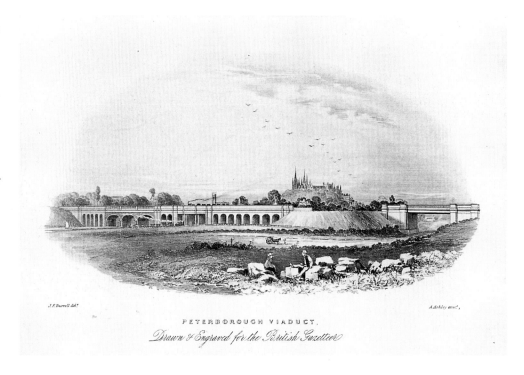

PETERBOROUGH VIADUCT,
Drawn & Engraved for the British Gazetteer

65 The Great Northern Station was built on the site of the old Sexton barn, the medieval tithe barn of the city, and opened in August 1850. It was a fairly simple design compared to the Gothic exuberances of many cities. One of the early visitors to the station was Charles Dickens who had a less than welcoming experience: 'The lady in the refreshment room was very hard on me, harder even than those fair enslavers usually are. She gave me a cup of tea, as if I were a hyaena and she my cruel keeper with a strong dislike to me. I mingled my tears with it, and had a petrified bun of enormous antiquity in miserable meekness.' The original station was demolished as unsafe in 1976 when the present more modern but featureless building was erected.

66　With so many railway lines entering Peterborough, level crossings caused problems, particularly as the town expanded and road traffic built up. One of the most notorious was the crossing of Cowgate/ Thorpe Road just before the lines entered North Station. Here the Great Northern lines ran parallel with the Midland Railway lines making a road crossing of over six lines. Each company had their own set of crossing gates with an area of 'no man's land' in between. Accidents were frequent and, following a tragic fatality in 1881, a pedestrian subway was built under both lines. This picture shows the Crescent Subway in the 1890s with two young men in their smart boaters marching purposefully into town whilst a family group emerges with dog, child and hoop in tow.

67   Eventually the present Crescent Bridge was built in 1913, taking its name from a row of desirable terrace houses which stood nearby and subsequently demolished. This popular local postcard of 1913, entitled 'Three Ways', shows all three ways to cross the railway line – the level crossing gates, the subway, and the new bridge.

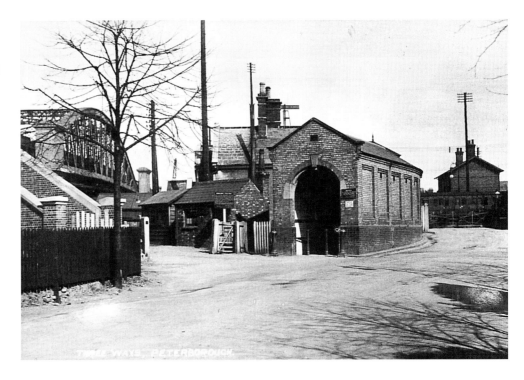

68 This nostalgic picture of the days of steam shows Crescent Bridge from the driver's perspective as he approaches North Station from the south. The joys of steam have been preserved in Peterborough by Nene Valley Railways, who operate on part of the old Blisworth branch line from Fair Meadow to just beyond Wansford.

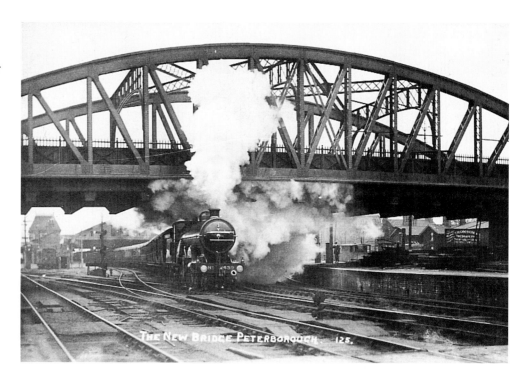

69   The approach to the North Station before the building of Crescent Bridge was originally at the end of Cowgate, forming an angle with St. Leonard's Street. Here we see the junction at the turn of the century with the Royal Temperance Hotel in the distance. Even in those days there was a need to warn against felonious activities. St. Leonard's Street has been replaced by the busy Bourges Boulevard inner ring road.

70   The other main mode of transportation for goods and people before the railway era and, as far as local traffic was concerned, well into the 20th century, was horse-drawn. This splendid example of rural transport, posed against the backdrop of the Cathedral, is carrying iron guttering and clay roof tiles. It stands outside H.B. Vergette's ironmongers shop in Cathedral Square a little before 1910. H.B. Vergette was the brother of Alderman Charles Vergette, founder of the prominent firm of local estate agents and auctioneers, and he had a reputation as one of the city's leading practical jokers. He also developed a plant nursery in Wellington Street from 1901. Both nursery and ironmongers shop closed in 1924.

71   The railway greatly increased the inflow of people to Peterborough and the city rapidly developed. However, there were many villages not on the railway system and they still had to rely on the horse-drawn carrier's carts. These were four-wheeled vans, usually with a wooden top, rather larger than a traditional gypsy wagon. Access was from the front, with seats along each side for the passengers. They averaged a little over two miles an hour for many journeys. On Wednesdays and Saturdays they clattered into Peterborough for the Market, stabling their horses at the numerous hostelries in the city. Here we see one such cart, minus its horse, at the Exchange Street end of Cumbergate in the 1890s. Keech's Toilet Saloon, being prepared for demolition, was one of several hairdressing saloons owned by this family in the town centre.

72   Horse-drawn omnibuses were advertised from 1857 with such distinctive names as 'The Champion' and the 'Baden Powell'. In 1896 William Bailey, auctioneer, valuer and landlord of the *Swan* in Midgate inaugurated The Peterborough Omnibus Company with a fleet of omnibuses and sixty horses plying between Long Causeway, Werrington, New England, Woodston, Fletton, Stanground, Farcet and Longthorpe. The horses were changed every two hours at the *Salmon and Compass* and the *Talbot* in Long Causeway. Here we see one of the omnibuses visiting or on display at the Peterborough Showground in Millfield.

73 Whenever a new mode of transport is introduced there is usually a period when the old and the new exist side by side, as here in Long Causeway between 1903 and 1905. The two appear to be competing in the Long Causeway Handicap and are neck and neck as they approach the tape.

74 The first electric trams were introduced by the Peterborough Electric Tram Company in 1903, with lines running from Cathedral Square to Walton, Dogsthorpe and Newark. It was not possible to run trams to the south of the city because of the difficulties encountered by Narrow Street and the Town Bridge. There were twelve trams, each with slatted wooden seats below and an uncovered deck above. Here the seats were reversible so that you could face either way. Two more trams were added in 1906 and the service continued until 1930, when the company was merged in the Eastern Counties Omnibus Company. In this picture we see a line of three trams at the Long Causeway terminus.

75   The demise of the tram was brought about eventually by the growth in the more flexible motorised transport, but there was a considerable period when they both overlapped. In this photograph bus and tram share the Market Place. The Electric Traction Company introduced charabancs in 1913 for running excursions and tours. The first trip was a circular tour of Castor, Wansford, Stamford and Market Deeping. By 1914 five were in operation to South Ward and nearer villages. Double-decker omnibuses were introduced in 1920s. The bus in this photograph is a 24 hp Straker Squire.

76   The first aeroplane to land in Peterborough was that of Mr. W.H. Ewen, a Scottish musician who touched down to admiring crowds in Mr. Hunt's field at Walton in June 1912. He had flown from St. Neots at 70-80 miles an hour in a 60 hp Caudron bi-plane. On landing he was presented with a silver rose bowl and a lucky silver horseshoe. The horseshoe proved effective for, after giving a series of displays over the weekend, he took off on Monday, 1st July, hit a tree and crashed. Fortunately he himself was unhurt, but the plane needed repair and it was several days later before he flew successfully to Lincoln.

Mr Ewen's Biplane after the accident at Peterboro' July 1st 12.

77   Until the mid-19th century Peterborough's economy was predominantly agriculture based, important amongst them being the milling of corn. There were three windmills in Peterborough, one in Thorpe Road, one at Millfield, and this post mill in Fengate. It was finally destroyed by fire in 1919.

78   The excuse for including this delightful porthole boating scene, if one was needed, is the building in the background. It is one of three steam driven mills built between 1840 and 1850 by the then Earl Fitzwilliam. It was leased to Michael Cadge and Samuel Colman in 1856. Colman came from the same family that set up the famous Colman's Mustard business.

79   Before 1990 Peterborough was lit by gas and much of the industry in the town was powered by gas engines. In spite of determined and lengthy opposition by the gas lobby, electricity finally came to Peterborough in 1900 with the opening of the first generating station on Albert Place Meadow, seen here around 1904.

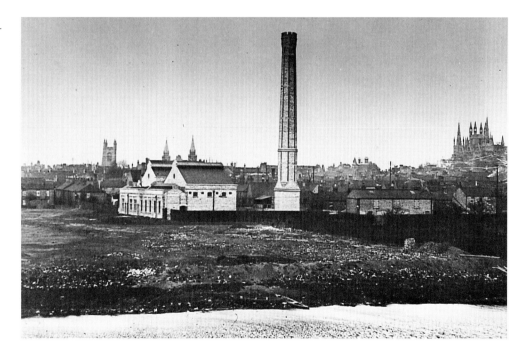

80 In 1884 a serious fire at the Peterborough Infirmary exposed the inadequacy of the existing city fire brigade. The Council decided to reorganise it, appointing (appropriately!) J.C. Gill, the waterworks engineer as Honorary Captain. At the same time a group of prominent businessmen formed the Peterborough Volunteer Fire Brigade who, for several decades maintained a rivalry with the city brigade, always seemingly one step ahead in introducing new practices and equipment. This photograph is of the city brigade about 1930 possibly on Armistice Day. At this time all the men were part-timers except for the captain, who lived in the fire station house which was located in a redundant Catholic Church premises in Queen Street.

81   The Peterborough Volunteer Fire Brigade, from the evidence of this photograph, obviously had a more laid back approach to fire-fighting. It was taken on safari to Guildford, probably at one of the many competitions in which the brigade took part, and were sometimes successful in winning. The Volunteer Brigade is still operational, working under contract to Cambridgeshire Fire and Rescue Service, providing 24-hour cover from its new headquarters off the Bourges Boulevard/Mayors Walk roundabout. In 1984 the Brigade was honoured with the Freedom of the City.

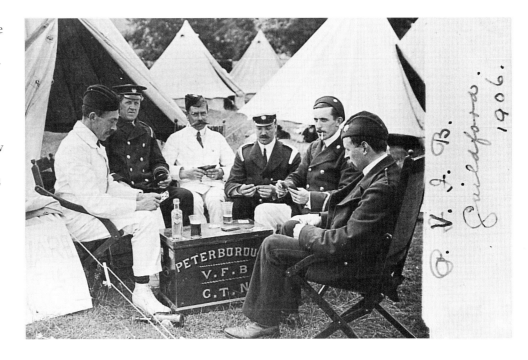

82 The city police force, shown here shortly after formation in 1874, consisted of a Chief Constable, two sergeants and seventeen men. The Chief Constable in the middle of the front row was probably James Hurst, who had been chief officer in the Liberty force. The Liberty force was controlled by the Magistrates and had previously been responsible for policing the city. In the early days of the city force there were disciplinary problems, with several constables being dismissed for drunkenness, one for incompetence, and one for falling asleep on his beat. The headquarters of the newly-formed force until 1949 were in Milton Street (now under Queensgate) in a house that was originally the Peterborough Infirmary.

83   Now we take a look at some of the ways in which Peterborians enjoyed themselves in days gone by. The river played an important part as a source of recreation. Here we see a group of boys in the 1890s taking a dip at the Town bathing place above River Lane in Woodston. The area was marked out by floating timbers and about a third of the river's width filled with gravel to provide a depth of two to four feet. Wooden cubicles were erected behind the towing path. It was open from May to September but was strictly for men and boys until a Ladies' Day was introduced in 1923.

84   Before the river was embanked, the surrounding open ground was flooded to a depth of a few inches every winter. All that was needed was a sharp frost to provide Peterborians with a ideal opportunity to 'get their skates on'. However, it was rare for the River Nene itself to freeze over but here is just such an occasion, taken from the Town Bridge. The chairs, which were hired out, served two purposes, firstly to enable skaters to sit when putting on and taking off their skates, and secondly for learners to push in front of them to keep their balance. On the extreme right of the photograph can be seen a Fenland lighter marooned outside English Brothers timber yard.

85   Rowing and canoeing were popular pastimes on the river and here we see a view of Peterborough Rowing Club's boathouse in the early 1880s. The club was founded in the mid-1870s and continued until the outbreak of the First World War. It appears from the photograph that the Club in those days encompassed both rowing and canoeing. The boathouse was demolished when the Rivergate Centre was built in the 1980s.

86   It is rare to see sailing boats on the Nene these days but earlier in the century it was a familiar sight. Partly visible to the right of the photograph is a houseboat, again a fairly common sight on the Nene at this time.

RIVER NENE, PETERBOROUGH

87 Not surprisingly, with such a flat terrain surrounding it, cycling was a popular pastime locally. The Peterborough Bicycle Club, formed out of an amalgamation of the Amateur Cycling Club and the Tricycle Club in 1875, is believed to be the oldest cycling club in existence. Here we see the Club on an outing to Lilford Hall.

88   Initially, Peterborough Cycling Club was for men and the women formed their own Ladies Cycle Club in 1893 to much public abuse. It met at the Bedford Hotel in Queen Street with Miss Goodman as captain. Women cyclists had to wear long skirts in town and this was a great hindrance but, once in the country, they took them off until the next village. This photograph may show the start of one of their outings, as they gather on the corner of Long Causeway and Cathedral Square. The Ladies Cycle Club was abandoned in 1898 when they joined the men, supposedly for greater safety!

89 Football has always been popular in Peterborough and flourished on an amateur basis from the 1870s. This photograph of the Peterborough City Football Club of 1910-11 was taken in front of their Crawthorne Road pavilion. It was one of the most famous sides in the early history of Peterborough football. In the 1911-12 season they set up a Club record by reaching the 4th qualifying round of the English cup. Peterborough City, who played in the Southern League, amalgamated with the most successful local club, Fletton United, in 1924 and later became the present professional side Peterborough United ('Posh').

90   Opinions are divided nowadays on the ethics of hunting but in bygone days the appearance of the Fitzwilliam Hunt was a popular event in Peterborough life. Here we see the Hunt setting off from the Fitzwilliam Stables in the 1920s.

91   Fairs were always an eagerly awaited event, both for entertainment and commerce. Peterborough Bridge Fair was founded in 1439 when Henry VI gave the Abbot permission to hold an annual fair on St. Matthew's Day (21 September) and the two following days 'at the bridge of Peterborough by the river Nene, as well in the County of Huntingdon as in the County of Northampton, on all sides of the bridge'. The fair has always been opened by proclamation. After morning prayers a procession was formed by the notables of the city and the proclamation was read at the fairground by the Town Crier. It is difficult to associate this dignified procession with having a good time at the fair. You expect them to be wearing 'Kiss Me Quick' hats and carrying balloons.

92   Here we see the good citizens of Peterborough streaming over the bridge into Oundle Road to enjoy 'all the fun of the fair'. Bridge Fair was usually a signal for bad weather. Its proximity to the river often meant that it was completely flooded or several inches deep in mud. By the 1880s its value as a trading centre had declined and it became more and more the pleasure fair we know today.

93 Part of the annual Bridge Fair in September included exhibits of wild animals by several menageries. Here we see Sanger's elephants, accompanied by a retinue of excited children, passing the Commercial Hotel in Cowgate on their way from the Great Northern Station to Fair Meadow on the south west bank of the river.

94 Charity events were also an opportunity for people to enjoy themselves, as in this picture of a young Edwardian lady trying to extract money for the Hospital Saturday Fund from two handsome gentlemen in Church Street around 1913. At least that's her story! The fund had an annual collection in order to raise funds for the maintenance and running costs of the hospital.

95 For a more quiet and relaxed means of recreation the citizens of Peterborough could always retire to the Town Park. The park, located about half a mile north of the town centre between Park Road and Broadway, was laid out in the 1870s. This picture of the Children's Corner and Bandstand was taken in the 1930s.

96   The Hippodrome, Broadway opened in 1907 and was sold a year later to a company controlled by Fred Karno. Many famous Music Hall stars appeared here including Charlie Chaplin and Marie Lloyd. Renamed *Palladium* in 1922 and *The Palace* in 1924 when it was bought by the Bancroft family. It doubled as a cinema from 1909 onwards and closed in 1937 when the Bancrofts opened *The Embassy* on adjoining land. A garage operated on the site until 1979, when it was cleared to make way for Tesco's Supermarket.

97   Theatre Royal, Broadway in the 1890s. The building began life in 1872 as a public hall with a frontage on Park Road. The owner W.D. Nichols, a local wine merchant and developer, adapted it for theatrical performances from 1878 and it was rebuilt as the *Theatre Royal* with an entrance to Broadway in 1894. Occasional films were put on as part of other shows and the cinema side expanded when the lease was obtained by the Palais-de-Luxe Company of London in 1910. In 1916 it was renamed *The Grand* and from then on ran with mainly touring plays. A further change of owner and name took place in 1919, this time being called *The Empire*, and it became the home of various touring repertory companies until closure in 1959. The building was demolished in 1961 for the erection of Shelton's department store, which itself was closed in the 1980s and converted into office accommodation.

98   Broadway post-1913, showing the *Broadway Kinema*, the *Hippodrome* and Brainsby's garage. The *Broadway Kinema*, Peterborough's first purpose built cinema, opened on 17th December 1910 as the *Broadway Electric Theatre*, seating some 700 people. Alterations were made in 1912 and it re-opened in 1913 as the Broadway Kinema, with 1000 seats. By the 1920s the 'Kinema' bit had been dropped and it was known as just *The Broadway*. Talkies came along in 1929 with Hitchcock's *Blackmail* one of the first to be shown. In 1959, the Rank Organisation, which now owned the building, officially changed the name to *Gaumont*. But it didn't last much longer as a cinema and was converted into a Bingo Hall in 1963. The building was demolished in 1987 and rebuilt as an amusement arcade and shops.

Broadway, Peterborough

99   Even those who are not members of the Salvation Army can get pleasure from listening to the public appearance of their Band, particularly at Christmas time. The Salvation Army came to Peterborough in 1883, meeting in a variety of venues, including the Temperance Hall, a paint shop, a pea factory, and the Drill Hall, before getting permanent premises in King Street. The Army now meets in modern premises off Bourges Boulevard. In the early days an opposition group, calling itself the 'Skeleton Army', tried to disrupt services and legal action had to be taken to restrain them. The first Salvation Army Band in Peterborough was formed in 1888 and the one shown here is that of 1908.

100   Now we look at some of the events, large and small, that made the news in Peterborough. Queen Victoria's Jubilee celebrations in 1897 provided an opportunity for the city to let its hair down. Here, in Cathedral Square, a camera-shy crowd turn their backs on the photographer to concentrate on the passing procession. The celebrations included a dinner of cold meats, hot potatoes and plum pudding for 1,200 poor people and, later, a tea for 5,000 schoolchildren, who each received a memento mug. During the day the schoolchildren were marched to the Market Place, where they sang to the vast crowds in the torrid heat. There was also a Regatta on the Nene.

101 Part of the Jubilee celebrations in 1897 included a 'monster procession' of vehicles from the Market Place to the Showground in Millfield. The vehicles were decorated to illustrate the trades of the city. Here we see an attractively decorated dog-cart proceeding past the *Crown Inn* and Webb, Webb & Co., provision merchants, in Westgate.

102　A curious crowd surveys the aftermath of a fire which gutted the Baptist Chapel in Queen Street in 1905. The chapel had been built in 1872 to replace an earlier one in Westgate. With some exaggeration the local press described the disaster as 'No Pompeian tragedy was ever more complete.' The Church met for over a year at the *Theatre Royal* in Broadway until the present building in Park Road was opened (see illustration 45).

103   General elections at the end of the last century and the beginning of this century were often much more tempestuous affairs than they are now. This picture records a famous incident that took place in the aftermath of the 1906 election in Peterborough which had been won by the Liberal candidate, George Greenwood, in a landslide victory. The coach that brought him home was hijacked on its return by a gang of overenthusiastic supporters who set it alight and dragged it flaming around the city centre. Several people occupying an increasingly hot seat on the roof, managed to escape unharmed. The gang finally dragged the coach into Narrow Street and attempted to push the remains into the porch of the Angel Hotel (a centre for Conservatism at that time), but is was too hot.

104   The events to mark the coronation of George V on 22nd June 1911 began in Peterborough at noon with the firing of a Royal Salute of twenty one guns by Peterborough Artillery on Fengate Recreation Ground. During the day there was a 'sumptuous dinner' for the old people of the city followed by entertainment at the *Hippodrome*; a singing of patriotic songs by a massed choir of 3,000 children in the Market Place; and, for the grown ups, a Coronation Pageant of vehicles on themes 'historical, emblematic, humorous, and utilitarian'. Here, in this picture, the pageant makes its way down Broad Bridge Street towards the Market Place. In the evening there was entertainment and dancing in the Park, attended by an estimated crowd of 15,000 people.

105   There was a particularly bad flood in Peterborough in August 1912 when the Nene rose 8 feet (2.4 metres) above its normal level. There are many photographs of its effect in different parts of the city. This is of cottages in Bodger's Yard, which was located at the rear of William Bodger's shop in Broad Bridge Street. Here the marooned inhabitants have used their initiative to construct a precarious walkway from planks and ladders. The local newspaper described the floods as 'this black week of rain and ruin'. One day it rained non-stop from 5.30 a.m. to 7 p.m.

106   Industrial relations could also be turbulent, as in this scene in 1913, when forty foundrymen at the Great Northern Railway engineering works in Westwood Street came out on strike following the dismissal of a moulder for throwing a blank cartridge into a hot ladle. The 'blacklegs' who remained at work were followed each day to and from work by the strikers, and bombarded with rude remarks. There was an attempt to make the stoppage national, but it was not sanctioned by the National Union of Railwaymen and the trouble gradually died down.

107 The outbreak of the First World War brought over excitement and anti-German fever to Peterborough. On 9th August 1914 an angry mob smashed the windows of two shops belonging to Frederick Frank and Frederick Metz, both German-born pork butchers who had lived in the town a long time, and flung the food about the streets. Hams were used as footballs and sausages strung from the electric tram wires. As soon as the Mayor heard of the disturbance he dashed round on his bike, read the Riot Act to the mob and called up troopers from the Northamptonshire Yeomanry. In this picture the soldiers confront the rioters outside Frank's shop in Narrow Street.

108   Things soon calmed down and recruiting started the day after the First World War was declared. In the first months 600 men joined up. It was possible in those days for groups of volunteers from the same place to form what was referred to as 'Pals' battalions so that they could serve together. Alderman Whitsed got permission of the War Office for a Peterborough 'Pals' battalion of the Northamptonshire Regiment, which became known as Whitsed's Own or Whitsed's Light Infantry. In this picture we see another group of 'Pals', Werner's Own Regiment leaving for the Front. On this occasion the city does not seem to have had a problem with the German connections of the city engineering firm of Werner Pfleiderer and Perkins, later to become Baker Perkins.

109   As the Germans poured into Belgium, the people fled before them and were offered hospitality in Britain. The Mayor of Peterborough, Sir Richard Winfrey (founder of East Midland Allied Press) was asked to find homes for some of them. The Corporation took over some untenanted houses and converted them to hostels. This picture shows a group of Belgian refugees who came to Peterborough in 1914. They soon became self-supporting and when repatriated at the end of the war are said to have taken with them far more cash and kind than they had brought.

110   There were many charitable events back home to support the troops. Here in the Market Place on Saturday, 15th August 1914 we see Rose Maidens, Margery Ellis and Kathleen Batten, selling a rose to Mr. Howell in aid of the Prince's Fund. The novel fund-raising idea came from Richard Brown of the Peterborough business W. and J. Brown, who donated over 8,000 roses to the effort. Mr. Brown thought 'they might fetch five or six pounds'. The bevy of Rose Maidens, all dressed in white, were organised by the Mayoress and so successful were their charms that the citizens of Peterborough happily parted with £90 in all.

111   This sombre scene depicts the funeral cortège of Thomas Hunter leaving the Peterborough Infirmary (now the City Museum). His death on the last day of July 1916 touched the hearts of Peterborough people who dubbed him the 'Lonely ANZAC'. He came from Kurri-Kurri in New South Wales, Australia, and was a sergeant in the Australia and New Zealand Army Corps. Badly wounded in the spine at the Battle of the Somme, he was on his way to Halifax by Red Cross train when it stopped at Peterborough. Being too ill to travel further, he was taken off the train and died the next day in Peterborough Infirmary. A bronze plaque in his memory was placed in the Cathedral and his grave lies in Broadway cemetery.

112   During the war, in March 1916, a 24-hour blizzard hit Peterborough leaving a foot of snow and practically cutting off communications with the outside world. Trains stopped, tradesmen gave up their rounds and between sixty and seventy great duplex telegraph poles were brought down. This view is taken near the Walton tram terminus on Lincoln Road. There was very little injury but incalculable damage caused.

AFTER THE GREAT STORM AT WALTON, PETERBORO.
MARCH 28TH 1916.

113   Peace came in 1918, but it was not until 19th July 1919 that Peterborough celebrated with a huge parade in which every city organisation took part. Thousands poured through the city centre, blocking Broadway, Long Causeway and the Market Place on their way to the old Showground. Here we see the parade proceeding down a very congested Broadway.

114 In 1921 a memorial tablet, which had been placed on the birthplace of the 'Peasant Poet' John Clare in Helpston by Peterborough Museum Society, was unveiled. Many grandchildren and great-grandchildren of the poet were present. The President of the Society H.B. Hartley (father of novelist L.P. Hartley) unveiled the tablet, after which an address was given by poet Edmund Blunden. Blunden was one of the first to draw attention to the importance of John Clare and to transcribe his poetry from the original manuscripts. In this photograph of the unveiling party and guests, posed against Helpston village cross, Edmund Blunden is the one holding books on the front row, and to the left of him is J.W. Bodger, Honorary Secretary of the Museum Society (see illustration 52), and H.B. Hartley.

115   You are in bed, re-
covering from an operation,
the last thing you want is a
railway engine to drop in
for breakfast. But that is just
what happened to Mrs.
Coles on 14th August 1922.
A runaway Midland and
Great Northern Railway engine travelling at 40 miles
an hour dashed into the
buffers and carried them
away, finally coming to a
halt after demolishing the
east wing of the old
Stationmaster's House. Mrs.
Coles was badly cut and
bruised but otherwise unin-
jured, as was her 17-year
old daughter Gladys who
was said to have 'emerged
from the rubble with a
smile on her face'.

116   A rare visit to the Peterborough Show by the Prince of Wales (later Edward VIII and, after abdication Duke of Windsor) in 1923. He is accompanied by G.C.W. Fitzwilliam and watched by a nervous policeman. His visit was made as President of the Peterborough and National Hound Shows. The Prince arrived at the North Station by a train that was specially stopped for him. Every street was elaborately decorated and lined by cheering crowds. Two incidents marred the day, first a prize pig was struck and killed by a bolt of lightning and then, on the Prince's return from the Showground, an old army pensioner, who appeared to be begging, jumped on the running board of his car and had to be removed promptly by a nearby constable.

117 This huge easy chair was part of a parade that took place during Peterborough Civic Week in June 1929. The float was constructed by the local furniture firm of Watkins and Stafford. The week's celebrations had several purposes, they marked the four-fold enlargement of the city, the laying of a foundation stone for the new Town Hall by Prince George (one of the sons of King George V), the opening of an enlarged Electricity Power Station, and the provision of a children's wing at the Peterborough and District Memorial Hospital.

118   By the early 1900s the Guildhall had become inadequate for meetings of the expanding City Council and officers and staff were housed in a variety of buildings. The Council initially bought land on the corner of Midgate and Broadway with the intention of building a Town Hall and offices. As a temporary measure the corner was let out as shops on short leases but, by the 1920s, the site was recognised as being inadequate for its original purpose. An alternative scheme was proposed that included the much needed widening of Narrow Street and the building of a new Town Hall and civic offices.

The building was designed by E. Berry Webber and construction completed in the early 1930s. This photograph shows it shortly after completion.

119   The oldest school in Peterborough, King's School, was founded by Henry VIII in 1541. It was originally situated in Minster Precincts but by the late 19th century had outgrown the facilities. The Dean and Chapter in the 1880s bought land in Thorpe Road, opposite the Peterborough District Hospital, with the intention of building a new school. However, following the death of a boy on the level crossing, they decided to look for a safer spot, and exchanged the site for one in Park Road, where the present building was erected in 1885. Here we see the Tower and the Big School early in the 20th century.

The King's School, Peterborough. The Tower and Big School.

120 These laboratories at King's School, seen here about 1944, were provided at the personal expense of Walter Ernest Cross, Headmaster from 1909 to 1913. He had previously been science master at Whitgift School, Croyden, and introduced the teaching of science to King's. He resigned in 1913 to become Headmaster of Maidstone Grammar School.

121   The other main boys school in the city was Deacon's School, founded in 1721 by woolcomber Thomas Deacon. He left the proceeds of his farm at Willow Hall and other properties to educate poor boys of Peterborough and to apprentice them to a trade. Their uniform was cinnamon suits and grey stockings. When they became apprenticed, the boys received a Bible and another suit of clothes. The school was originally in Cowgate but, following its reorganisation in 1882 as a public middle class school, it moved to new premises in Crown Lane (renamed Deacon's Street and now under Queensgate). Here we see it before 1909 when additions were made to the building. The school continued to expand and took over two other properties in the town centre, before moving to the present site in Queens Gardens in 1960.

Deacon's School, Peterborough.

122   Peterborough High School for Girls was founded in the late 19th century as a private school, located in Park Road. It remained in these premises until 1935 when the school moved to its present site at Westwood House, Thorpe Road. For a time the school changed its name to Westwood House School, but has recently reverted to the original title.

High School for Girls, Peterborough.
General View Showing Two School Houses

123   Over the bridge and a few yards along Thorpe Road lies this fortified structure, modelled on a Norman castle. It was built between 1840 and 1842 as the town gaol, replacing the old Bishop's Prison in King's Lodging which was located just inside the Cathedral Gateway. It was used as a prison for only thirty six years; after 1878 prisoners were sent to Northampton or Cambridge. Later it was used as the headquarters of the Liberty of Peterborough police force, who were responsible for the Soke of Peterborough but not the city, and as a magistrates' court. This latter use gave it its present name of the Sessions House. When the new magistrates court was built in Bishops Road, the Sessions House became a restaurant and public-house containing some interesting legal and police exhibits.

This view dates from about 1904 when the view was softened by trees.

Peterborough, Sessions House, Thorpe Road.

124   In 1955 this was thought to be the oldest inhabited thatched cottage in the city. It was located in New Road, between the *New Inn* and the entrance to the Gas Works. The cottage subsequently burnt down and the *New Inn* was demolished to make way for the Boongate roundabout at the end of New Road.

125 This charming, rustic cottage stood on the corner of Eastfield Road and Princess Gardens until 1904 and was known by the unusual name of Frog Hall. But looks can be deceptive as, according to a contemporary writer, '…the place had a very unsavoury reputation. It was inhabited by squatters, gipsies and travellers and was one of the least desirable places in the neighbourhood.'

126   When the Great Northern Railway established engine sheds in New England in 1853, it was still in the country and they had to run a workmen's train morning and evening from Peterborough. Then in 1860 the company built 260 cottages next to the workshops and a school in 1864. These cottages were better than other houses in Peterborough at that time, having both piped water and gas. This modernity is said to be the source of the area's name of New England, it was a vision of the future. The railway company's directors also gave most of the money for the erection of St. Paul's Church on Lincoln Road in 1869. This view, taken at the turn of the century, shows the original Fountain that still stands at the Triangle formed between Lincoln Road, Bourges Boulevard and Maskew Avenue.

127 Until the present century, Dogsthorpe was a little rural hamlet taking its name from a Saxon called Dodde. Here it is looking suitably rural in the 1890s. In the centre of the photograph is the *Bluebell Inn* dating from 1665. The cottages on the left have been demolished but the inn is still there, as are the first thatched cottage on the right and one further down Welland Road to the right of the picture.

128   Continuing north from Dogsthorpe was a lane (now Fullbridge Road) leading to the village of Paston. You can still sit in the shade of this fine avenue of trees in front of Itter Park, described here, with some stretch of the imagination, as Paston Valley. Since the 1960s, Paston has undergone substantial housing development and is now an integral part of the city, bounded on the south by the Soke Parkway.

PASTON VALLEY, PETERBOROUGH.   P67.

129   Until the mid-19th century Walton was a hamlet of around two hundred inhabitants. Things changed with the coming of the railways and it became a station on the Midland line from Peterborough through Stamford to Leicester. In this picture of the *Plough Inn* at Walton at the turn of the century, the Lincoln Road is still looking as if it will peter out to become a track round the next bend. Gradually housing spread along the Lincoln Road towards the city to link up with New England but the major expansion of Walton did not take place until after the First World War. *The Plough* stood near the junction with Marholm Road. It subsequently burnt down and was replaced by *The Railway Inn* which itself no longer exists.

130 To the south of the city lie the two parishes of Orton Longueville and Orton Waterville, incorporated but not submerged within the city in 1974 or by the development of the Orton township in the 1980s. The first part of their names is said to be a corruption of Overton, referring to the position of the villages looking over the Nene valley, and the second part to two Norman knights who owned the parishes, one called Long and one Walter. Here we see Orton Waterville looking suitably idyllic towards the end of the 19th century.

131   Orton Longueville could boast the splendid Orton Hall, home of the Huntly family. It is possible that the lady in the photograph is the Marchioness of Huntly who died in 1893. She was a renowned amateur botanist, geologist and zoologist and was responsible for planting the famous avenue of Wellingtonia trees in the grounds of the Hall. She also found time to produce fourteen children in the space of nineteen years! The Hall was built mainly in 1835 to a design by G.H. Smith of London but incorporates work from the 16th or early 17th century, including a doorway from Fotheringhay Castle. In recent years Orton Hall has been used as a school for children with special needs and is now a hotel and restaurant.

132   The *Gordon Arms*, on the Oundle Road might well be described as a 'copycat' inn, since it is based on the design of the *Queen Elizabeth* in Sevenoaks, Kent. The 10th Marquess of Huntly was so struck by the pub that he sketched it and this was later used as the basis for the design of the *Gordon Arms*. The pub was originally located on a site near to Orton Hall but was moved to its present position, on the opposite side of the Oundle Road and nearer Peterborough, in the early 1800s. The present pub and restaurant incorporates elements of the older building.

133   The main lodge house to Milton Hall, Castor, seen here, was, according to architectural historian Nikolaus Pevsner, formerly an inn. It was also in part used by the Fitzwilliam family until 1897 to collect tolls twenty days before and after Peterborough's fairs and for crossing Milton Ferry Bridge. Daniel Defoe (of *Robinson Crusoe* fame) initially praised the Earl for building the bridge but changed his tune when charged ²⁄₆d (12½p) for crossing it by coach, describing it as 'the only half crown toll that is in Britain'. In the last few years the lodge house has been moved a few hundred yards up the hill to make way for the Castor bypass. The bridge still stands and leads into Ferry Meadows Country Park and you no longer have to pay a toll.

134   With some exaggeration, the famous diarist John Evelyn described this building as a 'stately palace'. It is, in fact, Thorpe Hall, which lies on rising ground off Thorpe Road, one mile to the west of the city centre. Thorpe Hall was built in 1653/54 by Oliver St. John, Chief Justice of Common Pleas in Cromwell's government of 1648. He was also the man responsible for ensuring that Peterborough kept its Cathedral and in return was given the adjoining Chapel of St. Mary. It is said that Thorpe Hall was built partly out of the ruins of that chapel and local Barnack stone. It remained in the St. John family until the baronetcy became extinct. The Hall is now a Hospice run by the Sue Ryder Foundation.

135   On the right of this photograph is Park House, which stands at the entrance to Thorpe Hall. The path leading off on the left hand side is now Audley Gate and further down can be seen the old Toll House. The presence of a horse omnibus in the picture dates it to the turn of the century.

136   Continuing westward from Thorpe Hall brought you to the village of Thorpe itself (now called Longthorpe). In spite of its proximity to the city centre and modern housing developments, the village has managed to retaining a rural atmosphere. In this early photograph, the young girl may be waiting expectantly for a delivery of mail from the postman.

Thorpe Village, Near Peterborough.

137   Longthorpe is also home to a unique historical monument, Longthorpe Tower, seen here at the turn of the century. The Tower was built about 1300 as an extension to an earlier house which lies behind it. The house dates from about 1263 and was probably built by William de Thorpe who also built Longthorpe Church at about the same time for Robert de Thorpe, Lord of the Manor. The Tower's uniqueness stems from contemporary wall paintings in the Great Chamber of the Tower of which there are no comparable examples of this date or completeness in England. They depict the contrast between the worldly and the spiritual life. In addition to biblical and secular images, the paintings include representations of local animals and birds.

87

138 In 1874 Newark, two miles east of Peterborough on the road to Thorney and Wisbech, was a small hamlet of 244 people, mainly employed in agricultural work. In that year a portion of the parish was incorporated into the city. The introduction of electric trams in 1903 and the construction of a branch line via Eastfield Road to Newark, helped to strengthen the link. Since the 1950s, Newark has become engulfed by housing development and the old village is now unrecognisable. This photograph of Oxney Road is a reminder of how it looked circa 1920. The village school can just be seen on the left hand side. The photographer who took this picture would now be standing in the middle of the busy Frank Perkins dual carriageway looking towards Sainsbury's car park and supermarket on the right.

139 Stanground, on the road to Whittlesey and Ramsey, is mentioned in the Domesday Book, although settlements in the area go back to prehistoric times. Its name may refer to the stony ground by the village as opposed to the fen land or to an ancient stone cross that marked the boundary with Fletton, and is now located in the churchyard. Stanground was also located on an important waterway that linked the Nene with, ultimately, the Great Ouse. In the early 1900s more than six gangs of Fenland lighters operated from there, as well as boatyards to carry out necessary repairs. The Staunch, seen in this photograph early in the century, was a safety valve on the waterway to prevent water from the Middle Level from flowing into the Nene. The cottage has now been replaced by a more modern building.

140 The village of Werrington, north of Peterborough, on the road to Lincoln has ancient roots. It was mentioned in early charters as a manor belonging to Peterborough Abbey as long ago as 1013. Parts of the church of St. John the Baptist date from the 12th century. Until 1853, however, it was part of the parish of Paston. In 1901 the population was 724; it is now around 20,000 and Werrington is attached to the city as a suburban township. The nucleus of the old village has survived and this picturesque thatched building is now the Cherry Tree Restaurant. In previous lives it has been a farmhouse, a boarding school, a doctor's surgery, a dairy and, at the time of this photograph, a village store and post office.

12. The Post Office, Werrington